CHOICES

ALIGNING YOUR CHOICES WITH THE LORD'S CHOICE

BY DAVID J. BALDWIN

ACKNOWLEDGMENT

T o Pastor Rich Pennington Jr.:
  Thanks for your ongoing support and guidance,
seeing this book rise from a thought to publication.

CONTENTS

Preface ix

Did God Really Say vs. God Did Say 1

Matured vs. Maturing 4

Silence vs. Praise 7

Natural Love vs. God's View on Love 10

Troubled vs. Joyful 13

Unforgiveness vs. Forgiveness 16

Lack of Control vs. Self-control 19

Who Cares vs. I Care 21

No One is Home vs. Answering the Door 23

Impatience vs. Patience 25

Boundaries vs. Unrestricted 28

Past vs. Present 30

My Way vs. God's Way 32

My Revenge vs. God's Wrath 35

Absorbing vs. Reflecting 38

Condemned vs. Forgiven 40

Panic vs. Calm 43

Minimum Effort vs. Going Beyond the
    Minimum 45

Tightfisted vs. Openhanded...............................48

Aimless vs. Purposeful 51

Fear vs. Courage 53

Sitting in the Bleachers vs. Taking the Field......56

Hidden vs. Seen 59

Discouragement vs. Encouragement 61

Separated vs. Together.......................................64

Worthless vs. Valuable 67

Consuming vs. Saving...70

Dissatisfied vs. Content 73

Misery vs. Mercy...75

Earthly Planning vs. Eternal Planning 78

Wants vs. Needs..80

Fairness vs. Unfairness 83

Silent vs. Confessed..85

Most of the Most vs. Least of the Least.............88

Shocked vs. Prepared...92

I Will Try vs. I Will 95

Well Said vs. Well Done 97

It's Your Choice to Make....................................99

PREFACE

"Be careful, however, that the exercise of your freedom does not become a stumbling block ..." (1 Corinthians 8:9)

God has given us free will to live our lives as we choose. He has advised us of boundaries to stay within, but it is our choice to stay within them. When choosing to live outside of God's boundaries we do so without God's will and in turn suffer from the consequences for such decisions.

In our hearts, we desire to do the right things while following the way of God; however, as we all know, we do fall short by making the wrong choices. The big culprit is the evil one, who is pushing temptations and worldly influences upon us. They are very powerful and very inviting. Since these worldly forces surround us daily, it is so important to think through our choices and how they match up with the Scriptures. This book is designed to help you with that in mind.

Will this book cover all of your choices? No, but it will give you a pattern to follow when reflecting upon your choices, which is to seek God's guidance, read the Scriptures, reflect upon your past actions by asking yourself some tough questions, make the necessary corrections, and then set the tone for making better decisions in the future.

This book is not designed as a quick read. Perhaps you can read one devotional a week and, throughout the week, reflect upon that devotional.

The key is to allow God ample time to give you clarity regarding your past choices and guidance on your future decisions.

"I have chosen the way of truth…" (Psalm 119:30)

My prayer is that your heart be open to God's Word, that these devotionals help you reflect upon your choices in life, and that your decisions will be in alignment with the Lord's choices.

To God be all the glory. Best of blessings to you!

Dave

DID GOD REALLY SAY VS. GOD DID SAY

*"Now the serpent was more crafty than any of the wild animals the Lord God had created. He said to the woman, '**Did God really say**, You must not eat from any tree in the garden?' The woman said to the serpent, 'We may eat fruit from the trees in the garden, but **God did say**, You must not eat fruit from the tree that is in the middle of the garden, and you must not touch it, or you will die.' 'You will not surely die,' the serpent said to the woman."* (Genesis 3:1-4)

It is so easy to read this and say "Eve, don't eat from that tree! Why are you even entertaining that thought? Why is this so difficult for you? Just stay away and stop being so careless. After all, don't you remember what *God did say?*" It's always easy to point out the sinful acts of others, but, due to the excuses we make, it's not so easy to recognize our own.

All of us have had our Eve moments. They begin with the serpent enticing us into a conversation that builds momentum to the point where we change what *God did say* to *what did God really say?* We cross the line when we create enough excuses to take a sinful act and convert it into what we believe is now an acceptable act.

Temptation is everywhere. It is the evil one's calling card, and he uses it to try to break our faith, break our relationship with God, and ruin our testimony. Being tempted is not the sin; acting upon the temptation is the sin. God has no part in sinful temptations – only the evil one does.

> *"When tempted, no one should say, 'God is tempting me.' For God cannot be tempted by evil, nor does he tempt anyone; but each one is tempted when, by his own evil desire, he is dragged away and enticed. Then, after desire has conceived, it gives birth to sin; and sin, when it is full-grown, gives birth to death."*
> (James 1:13-15)

When a sinful temptation is upon you, don't stay in a conversation with the serpent; the evil one is stronger than you. Stop talking, turn your back to the temptation, and run to God. He has the power to overcome all situations. It is our choice to make: either to act in a way that says *God did say* or to side-step the situation with *did God really say?*

Reflections:

- Do you guess what is right or wrong, or do you read the Scriptures to find out?
- Have you ever tried to persuade yourself that the Scriptures did not apply to a certain situation in your life, thus changing what *God did say* to *did God really say?*
- Do you recognize your conversations with the serpent? If you don't, be watchful because they do exist. Even Jesus had a conversation with the tempter. Read Matthew 4:1-11.
- Are you proactive in combating your temptations through prayer? Be ready to act before temptation knocks on your door.
- What is your spirit guiding you to pray for?

"Watch and pray so that you will not fall into temptation. The spirit is willing, but the body is weak." (Mark 14:38)

MATURED VS. MATURING

"… grow in the grace and knowledge of our Lord and Savior Jesus Christ. To him be glory both now and forever!" (2 Peter 3:18)

As part of the spiritual maturing process, we must educate ourselves regarding God's wisdom. The key word here is maturing, as opposed to having matured. Maturing is an ongoing process; it never ends. Until we have the knowledge and ability to create a universe, it would be wise to actively reach and grasp for all the wisdom God has in store for us so we can be the best we can be for the kingdom.

There is no arm-twisting here. If you really love the Lord, it only makes sense that you want to know more of His ways. Just as with a role model you admire, you want to know why and how they do what they do so you can learn from their experiences. If you are a true believer, you know the Lord's ways are all in the Scriptures, and from the Scriptures we learn.

If we are the same today as yesterday, then we have not grown. The goal is to be better than yesterday and even better tomorrow. Jesus is the only one who can say He was the *"...same yesterday and today and forever"* (Hebrews 13:8) because Jesus is perfect and we are not.

This world is full of challenges and temptations. As we grow in the knowledge of God, we become wiser. We are able to recognize and foil the tempter's challenges to bring us down and ruin our testimony. We see Peter encouraging Christians to add to their knowledge of the Lord because many false teachers distort the truth. It is our personal responsibility to know the truth. Too many Christians put *all* their spiritual education into the hands of their pastor. It is impossible for a pastor to teach everything one needs to know about the Scriptures. Also, how do we know that what they are teaching is correct if we don't even read the Scriptures? Sunday service has its place, but it is not the only place to be spiritually educated. It is our choice to keep maturing in the Word, with the motivation to learn as much as possible, or not.

"... let the wise listen and add to their learning ..." (Proverbs 1:5)

Reflections:

- Does your knowledge of the Scriptures increase every year?
- Do you set goals and/or have a plan for maturing spiritually? If not, what can you put into practice over the next few months as a means to keep you maturing spiritually?
- Do you allow yourself to be teachable? This will be evident in lifestyle changes.
- What is your spirit guiding you to pray for?

SILENCE VS. PRAISE

"David praised the Lord in the presence of the whole assembly, saying, 'Praise be to you, O Lord, God of our father Israel, from ever-lasting to everlasting. Yours, O Lord, is the greatness and the power and the glory and the majesty and the splendor, for everything in heaven and earth is yours. Yours, O Lord, is the kingdom; you are exalted as head over all. Wealth and honor come from you; you are the ruler of all things. In your hands are strength and power to exalt and give strength to all. Now, our God, we give you thanks, and praise your glorious name.'" (1 Chronicles 29:10-13)

D avid was a master of praising the Lord. We can learn and be inspired by his energy and ways of worshiping the Lord. As we read the Scriptures we can see why the Lord said David was *"a man after my own heart"* (Acts 13:22). David loved God and was not afraid to show his dependence upon Him and reverence for Him.

The opposite of praise is silence. The problem with silence is the lack of acknowledgment for who God is. Our silence expresses an unintentional or even willing divide. Our silence demonstrates a lack of total surrender. We break our silence through the recognition of who the Lord really is and what He means to our lives. Our heart will move into a realm of thankfulness and reverence, thus unleashing our praises upward to the heavens.

The bottom line is that you cannot be spiritually healthy through silence. Praise keeps one's heart mindful of whom we belong to. Such praise will keep us humble, keep us respectful, keep us thankful, keep us mindful, keep us fruitful, keep us guided, keep us watchful, keep us peaceful, keep us joyful, keep us faithful, keep us diligent, keep us generous, keep us rested, keep us strong, and keep us connected. All in all, the choice to praise will keep us properly aligned. Silence will only keep us dark and distant, and it is our choice to make.

"May my lips overflow with praise ..."
(Psalm 119:171)

Reflections:

- Where is your heart with regard to praising the Lord?
- Would you say your lips *overflow with praise* to the Lord on a regular basis?

- Do you feel that your level of praise to God is where it needs to be?
- What is your spirit guiding you to pray for?

"Let everything that has breath praise the Lord." (Psalm 150:6)

NATURAL LOVE VS. GOD'S VIEW ON LOVE

"Be imitators of God, therefore, as dearly loved children and live a life of love, just as Christ loved us and gave himself up for us as a fragrant offering and sacrifice to God."
(Ephesians 5:1-2)

For me, the best sensation in the world is being loved, knowing that a person will always be there for you and will love you no matter how poor you are, no matter how many times you mess up, and no matter how far you've wandered.

Such a love is recounted by Jesus in His parable about the young prodigal son who demanded his share of his father's estate. We see that the father divided the property between his two sons. The young son left home with his inheritance for a distant country and *squandered his wealth in wild living*. After a time, he returned home, broken financially and spiritually. You would think, quite naturally, that his father would chastise him for wasting his inheritance. However, the father *"saw him and was filled with compassion for him. He ran to his son, threw his arms around him, and kissed him."* After embracing his prodigal son, the father offered up a celebratory feast, because his son was *"dead and is alive again; he was lost and is found."*

So to be imitators of God's love, we must fully understand what encompasses God's supernatural love. We must also understand the differences between God's type of love versus natural love; otherwise we will never be able to fulfill our greatest commandment, to love (Mark 12:28-31).

God's love is an all-encompassing, unconditional, unfailing, unlimited, non-prejudicial, and everlasting love. In contrast, natural love is limited to and controlled by circumstances. An imperfect natural love is an easy type of love, because it is a selfish love. For example, this love only exists when all the conditions *we* have established are met. If any of these conditions that *we* have established are broken, this natural love can easily vanish. However, God's type of love is supernatural. It is a perfect love, an unselfish love that has no barriers to entry. It begins by putting the needs of others before our own. A true Christian who has felt the love of God will want to emulate this love. As an imitator of God's love, we will replace our natural love with supernatural love and bring honor and glory to God through our acts of supernatural love. Those who have received supernatural love will ask, "Where does such love come from?" Our response is to point upward to the heavens.

So we have a choice: to love naturally with limitations or to *be imitators of God's love*, which reaches to the heavens. God's love is a priceless love.

"How priceless is your unfailing love!" (Psalm 36:7)

<u>**Reflections:**</u>

- Does your love have worldly conditions?
- Would others view your love as a priceless love?
- Are you able to share God's love with someone who has harmed or wronged you?
- How can you be a better imitator of God's love to *all* – not just to those who are easy to love?
- What is your spirit guiding you to pray for?

TROUBLED VS. JOYFUL

"Be joyful always, pray continually; give thanks in all circumstances, for this is God's will for you on Christ Jesus." (1 Thessalonians 5:16)

This Scripture inspires us to be joyful and thankful in all circumstances. This is easy during the sunny seasons of our life, but it is difficult to express the spirit of joy during the darkest of seasons when one's spirit is not grounded in Christ Jesus. If your faith is entangled with earthly influences, you will have a difficult time relaying spiritual joy when times get tough. When we are able to disentangle ourselves from the natural and raise our hands to the supernatural, God brings us a peace that helps soothe any pain our spirit is feeling, and for that we are blessed.

"…for the joy of the Lord is your strength." (Nehemiah 8:10)

My first real test of faith came when my mom died. To this day, she is the most precious person who has ever touched my life. When God called her home, I had to get real with my faith and ask, "Do I really believe in all that I said I believed?" Through my tears, I concluded yes. I found myself at peace even in the midst of the saddest, most painful day of my life. To some degree I felt I had truly cemented my belief in God. Up to this point I had all this intellectual knowledge of God, but my mom's death tested the core of my soul. The result was that I was able to find joy in the strength of the Lord, because I knew where Mom was. I knew she was no longer in pain, I knew she was reunited with her mother, whom she missed greatly, and I knew that one day we would be together again for all eternity.

If your joy seems to fluctuate, then it is tied to the natural. If this is the case, your joy is trapped by boundaries, restrictions, and limitations of earthly circumstances. In contrast, spiritual joy is liberating. It has no boundaries, and no earthly circumstance can suppress it or claim it. Spiritual joy knows that God is in control, and for that we can rest and be in peace. When others see that our joy is uninhibited by our earthly circumstances, they will witness that our message of hope in Christ Jesus is consistent with our walk with the Lord.

Reflections:

- Are there any earthly obstacles holding onto your spirit of joy?
- Through you, do others witness the spirit of joy in Christ Jesus?
- During dark times, are you able to share spiritual joy?
- What is your spirit guiding you to pray for?

"A cheerful heart is good medicine..."
(Proverbs 17:22)

UNFORGIVENESS VS. FORGIVENESS

Stoned with Forgiveness

"While they were stoning him, Stephen prayed, 'Lord Jesus, receive my spirit.' Then he fell on his knees and cried out, 'Lord, do not hold this sin against them.'" (Acts 7:59-60)

What a forgiving spirit Stephen had! Take a moment to put yourself in his situation. Imagine each rock being hurled at you, and the pain of each stone impacting your body. It is amazing that during all the agony Stephen experienced, he still managed to put the needs of others first. Stephen recognized that the stone casters were not spiritually guided individuals and thus needed help. Proverbs 4:19 puts such darkness within people in these terms:

"... the way of the wicked is like deep darkness; they do not know what makes them stumble."

Recognizing the stone casters' need for help, Stephen offered up a prayer of forgiveness similar to the prayer Jesus offered while on the cross.

"Jesus said, 'Father, forgive them, for they do not know what they are doing.'" (Luke 23:34)

We all know that clogged arteries limit our physical ability to function at our best. Our spiritual heart suffers from clogging as well. When we cannot extend forgiveness to others, it limits our ability to serve God as He intended. It is our choice to either forgive as God taught or to harbor the darkness of not forgiving.

"Get rid of all bitterness, rage and anger, brawling and slander, along with every form of malice. Be kind and compassionate to one another, forgiving each other, just as in Christ God forgave you." (Ephesians 4:31-32)

Reflections:

- Does your forgiveness policy have boundaries or limitations?
- Is your forgiveness policy in alignment with the Scriptures?

- Do you need to make any changes to your forgiveness policy?
- Is there someone, dead or alive, for whom you are withholding forgiveness? If so, can you look beyond the pain and consider the possibility of forgiveness? Forgiveness may not take place immediately, but at least put it to prayer and ask God to reveal His will.
- What is your spirit guiding you to pray for?

LACK OF CONTROL VS. SELF-CONTROL

"Like a city whose walls are broken down, is a man who lacks self-control." (Proverbs 25:28)

In the Old Testament, city walls were used to protect the inhabitants from passing groups of marauders. Without these walls, the inhabitants would be subject to attack. Well, God's commands are our walls. As we stay within God's walls, we remain under His protection. Now God does not set up these boundaries to limit our joy in life. God sets up these boundaries because He loves us and wants to protect us from the difficulties we will face when we leave the security of His walls. Throughout the Scriptures we see where people have suffered greatly for their lack of self-control in following God's ways, just like a city without walls.

The way I see it, we are given an opportunity to choose from one of two steering wheels for our lives: an earthly wheel or a Spirit-filled wheel. The earthly wheel confuses your mind into believing you have control of your life and are fully protected, a mental mirage. In reality, you have no real protection because you are steered by earthly circumstances over which you have no control. However, if we choose the Spirit-filled wheel, we grasp the reality that we are controlled by the hands of God. Under such protection, like that of a secured city, we are no longer influenced by earthly circumstances because we are only influenced by the ways the Spirit moves us.

> *"Blessed is the man who makes the Lord his trust…"* (Psalm 40:4)

Reflections:

- How self-controlled are you to be able to stay within God's walls?
- The evil one tries to create environments that test our ability to remain self-controlled in God's ways. Is there anything in your life that is lacking self-control?
- How easily are you affected by earthly circumstances? If you are easily affected, you may need to check for some damage to your city walls.
- What is your spirit guiding you to pray for?

WHO CARES VS. I CARE

"Therefore, as God's chosen people, holy and dearly loved, clothe yourselves with compassion, kindness, humility, gentleness and patience." (Colossians 3:12)

In the fashion world, clothing styles change every season. What you buy today will not be in fashion next year.

Being clothed in *compassion, kindness, humility, gentleness,* and *patience* is not to be compared to the fashion world, which changes all the time. We must wrap ourselves in these qualities of goodness in a supernatural way, a way that is seen by everyone and never goes out of style.

Natural ways of goodness are easy for us to follow because they have preset limitations. However, our natural ways stop when we are born again, because we have received the Holy Spirit. The Holy Spirit empowers us with divine goodness. The problem arises when human nature begins to battle with divine nature. During such a time, human nature can kick in and not represent the goodness of God. Paul's letter to the Colossians inspires us to be clothed in divine goodness at all times and for all people. Doing so is not always easy and at times can be uncomfortable – a natural response – but in our heart we must choose the right thing to do in order to honor God – a divine response.

As believers, we are not the same as we were prior to our confession of faith. We are empowered to go beyond the natural. We are new people in Christ, changed people who make others say, "I want what they have." Thus, we spread the message of hope to those who don't know Christ. If we have not changed after our confession of faith, then we have chosen to be just another person blending into the crowd.

Reflections:

- Are your traits of compassion, kindness, humility, gentleness, and patience limited to those with whom you get along, or are they *evident to everyone*?
- In times of conflict do you remain clothed in God's ways of goodness?
- What is your spirit guiding you to pray for?

NO ONE IS HOME VS. ANSWERING THE DOOR

"Here I am! I stand at the door and knock. If anyone hears my voice and opens the door, I will come in and eat with him, and he with me." (Revelation 3:20)

I don't know about you, but one of my pet peeves is salespeople who cold call, knocking on everyone's door in the neighborhood. You open the door, they say their spiel, you politely say no, but they have more to say and want to become your buddy. I may be over exaggerating a little, but when I'm home, I just want to relax. I don't want to be interrupted.

Now my confession is on the table, and I wonder how many times all of us do such a thing to God, unintentionally of course. For example, "Oh man, I just don't want to be interrupted right now." Or, "Things are really busy, and I just can't answer the door right now." Or, "I'm sorry, but I am just too comfortable to get off the couch and answer the door."

To hear God's voice, one has to be motivated to hear His knock first and then open the door. In Revelation 3, we see that the Laodicean church was not available. They became complacent and entangled in their earthly pleasures. This caused them not to feel Christ's presence. You could say Christ knocked on their heart, but no one was home.

The bottom line is that we need to be cognizant of how our earthly belongings and circumstances distract us from seeking and being available to God. We should make the choice to ask ourselves on a regular basis, "How available have I been lately?"

"God looks down from heaven on the sons of men to see if there are any who understand, any who seek God." (Psalm 53:2)

Reflections:

- How available have you been to hear God's knock and answer the door?
- Do you *regularly* allocate enough time to listen for God?
- What can you use as a reminder to ask yourself the question, "How available have I been lately?"
- What is your spirit guiding you to pray for?

"I love those who love me, and those who seek me find me." (Proverbs 8:17)

IMPATIENCE VS. PATIENCE

"Wait for the Lord and keep his way." (Psalm 37:34)

Most of us have had a moment where we acted too hastily and thought, *Had I only waited this would not have happened. What was I thinking?* The big culprit is lack of patience. Our impatience is very dangerous, as it can take us unintentionally down some very dark paths.

I wonder if Abraham had such a "what was I thinking?" moment after finally having a child with his wife Sarah. He and Sarah believed that she was barren, even though God promised Abraham a son who would inherit his estate. So Abraham had a child with his maidservant. This created all kinds of problems between Sarah, Hagar, and the two children. All of this would have been prevented if Abraham waited for God's timing.

Patience is a spiritual discipline that battles the earthly desire for instant results. The key is to keep watch for such moments and monitor our patience level so that there is no interference with God's timing.

A great story about honoring God's timing is that of Noah. After spending many months at sea, and an entire year inside the ark, Noah waited on God to tell him when to come out of the ark (Genesis 8:3-16). Noah had such incredible patience waiting for God. I'd like to think that I would have such patience, but someone would probably have to chain me down in order for me to stay on that ark after it docked.

It is easy to say we want to honor God's timing, but converting such thoughts into action can be difficult at times. However, as difficult as it may be, we should choose not to run ahead of God. Such intentions need to be in our prayers, asking God to give us the strength not to get ahead of Him. There is only one timeline to follow and that is God's timeline. Making every effort to throw away our timeline will bring to a final standstill those frustrating moments of "what was I thinking?"

Reflections:

- Do you allow room for God's timing?
- Do you pray for God's will and timing to override your will and your timing?
- How is your level of patience in waiting for God's timing?

- Is there an area of your life in which you may be moving ahead of God's timing?
- What is your spirit guiding you to pray for?

> *"Since ancient times no one has heard, no ear has perceived, no eye has seen any God besides you, who acts on behalf of those who wait for him."* (Isaiah 64:4)

BOUNDARIES VS. UNRESTRICTED

"Jabez cried out to the God of Israel, 'Oh, that you would bless me and enlarge my territory! Let your hand be with me, and keep me from harm so that I will be free from pain.' And God granted his request." (1 Chronicles 4:10)

When one builds a house, its size is limited by its foundation. When we submit our prayer requests, it is best not to erect a boundary or set limits. We have a mighty God who does mighty things, so why set limits for our prayers? For example, if you are praying for your ministry to reach ten people, pray to reach a *minimum* of ten people. God did say ask and you shall receive. If you ask for ten, He just may give you ten, and you probably would feel good about that. But what about the day you give an account of your life, and Jesus says, "Remember that day you asked to reach ten people? I gave you ten, but I also had another fifteen to be reached." I don't know if such a conversation will occur, but why take a chance? I would rather expect more than less, thus providing God the opportunity to go beyond any predetermined expectations. The only limitations are the ones we choose to set for ourselves. We need to be careful how we pray so that our prayers are not limited to our expectations.

Jabez's prayer is a good example of not creating boundaries around prayer requests. We see Jabez requesting that his territory be enlarged. Jabez allowed God to determine by how much. Jabez did not say give me a certain city, or enlarge my territory another twenty miles; he just said enlarge my territory and allowed God to do the rest.

<u>Reflections:</u>

- Have you put boundaries around any of your prayer requests?
- When you pray, do you give God a chance to display all of His abilities?
- Are your prayers reflective of an almighty God?
- What is your spirit guiding you to pray for?

PAST VS. PRESENT

"The crowd joined in the attack against Paul and Silas, and the magistrates ordered them to be stripped and beaten. After they had been severely flogged, they were thrown into prison, and the jailer was commanded to guard them carefully. Upon receiving such orders, he put them in the inner cell, and fastened their feet in the stocks. About midnight Paul and Silas were praying and singing hymns to God, and the other prisoners were listening to them." (Acts 16: 22-25)

This Scripture is a great example of how the past should not have a life of its own. Later that evening, after being *stripped* and *severely beaten,* Paul and Silas prayed and sang hymns to God. Their actions led a jailer and his family to the Lord. Paul and Silas refused to allow the past to keep on living.

"Forgetting what is behind, and straining toward what is ahead, I press on toward

the goal to win the prize for which God has called me heavenward in Christ Jesus." (Philippians 3:13-14)

Living in the past is nothing but a headwind into the future. *Living* in the past has no value, although *learning* from the past does. Today has life, tomorrow has life, but the past is gone; so let the past sleep. It is your choice to make!

Reflections:

- Is there anything from your past that still has life today? If so, what can you start doing today in order to put the past to sleep forever?
- Is there anything from your past that can be used as a testimony to your faith in God?
- Are you able to *pray and sing hymns to God,* even in your darkest of seasons?
- Has anything from the past dampened your relationship with God? If so, consider seeking godly counsel to help bring closure to this matter.
- What is your spirit guiding you to pray for?

MY WAY VS. GOD'S WAY

"I will instruct you, and teach you in the way you should go; I will counsel you, and watch over you. Do not be like the horse or the mule, which have no understanding but must be controlled by bit and bridle or they will not come to you." (Psalm 32:8-9)

One of Frank Sinatra's famous songs was "My Way." Some of the lyrics are,

I planned each charted course;
Each careful step along the byway,
But more, much more than this,
I did it my way.

It's a great song, but not the way God wants us to live our life. Sadly, there are many who declare their faith in God, but their actions are more like this song; they are living life their way.

God has a longing to love us, to teach us, to guide us, and to protect us. However, when we live life our way, we cancel all of this. We are not to live life in a way that feels good to us. We are to live a life as offered by the Creator. This begins with knowing the Scriptures, which are the backbone of living life God's way. Unfortunately, many Christians have neglected the Scriptures. Misguided, they set their own rules by believing that if they live a "good life" everything will be OK. God is the Creator of all, and He gave us a blueprint to follow – the Scriptures. So if the Scriptures are not being read, then how can you possibly know if you are living a *good life*? It's like playing the game of golf without ever reading the *Rules of Golf*. If that is the case, how do you know if you are keeping score properly? How do you know what penalties to assess when you do not even know what the infractions are?

The bottom line is that we need to educate ourselves on God's ways and not assume we know His ways. As we educate ourselves, we must apply this knowledge to our actions. Knowledge without action makes no sense; it's a choice to make.

"Lead me, O Lord, in your righteousness... make straight your way before me." (Psalm 5:8)

Reflections:

- Is there anything in your life you may be doing your way instead of God's way?
- Do you find yourself to be more self-reliant than God-reliant?
- Do you *regularly* seek God to lead you?
- What is your spirit guiding you to pray for?

MY REVENGE VS. GOD'S WRATH

"If it is possible, as far as it depends on you, live at peace with everyone. Do not take revenge, my friends, but leave room for God's wrath, for it is written: 'It is mine to avenge; I will repay,' says the Lord." (Romans 12:18-19)

God can handle revenge more efficiently than we can. At the moment of wanting to exact revenge, acting upon that emotion can only make matters worse. Compare this to a doctor who should not operate on his own child because his emotions may interfere with the surgery. When feelings of revenge arise, we must choose to let God handle the circumstances His way. After all, the Lord did say, *"It is mine to avenge...."* God knows what happened, and He will take care of what needs to be taken care of, in His timing. For that, we say amen and yield to God.

It can be difficult to turn away from exacting revenge. So much pain and pent-up emotion needs to be released. However, we must follow the Scriptures by stepping aside and allowing room for God to move ahead of us so that He may fulfill His will and His purpose for that situation.

> *"Do not say, 'I'll pay you back for this wrong!' Wait for the Lord, and he will deliver you."* (Proverbs 20:22)

Being mistreated is inevitable. All of us will be exposed to such situations throughout our lifetime; some may even be dreadfully painful. We must handle such events spiritually, not emotionally. It's a choice for us to make.

Reflections:

- Do you have enough faith in God to allow Him to handle a revengeful situation?
- Is there currently a situation in which you may be intentionally or even unintentionally trying to get revenge?
- Has anything occurred in the past to which you applied revenge? If so, how do you feel about that today? Based on God's Word, how would you handle that differently today?
- Is there someone in your path who is planning revenge? Is God leading you to share His wisdom?

- What is your spirit guiding you to pray for?

  "May my vindication come from you; may your eyes see what is right." (Psalm 17:2)

ABSORBING VS. REFLECTING

"It is not good to eat too much honey, nor is it honorable to seek one's own honor." (Proverbs 25:27)

Over the years, many athletes have cheated to win. In 1980, there was the famous controversy of a marathon runner who appeared to have won the race. However, questions arose because she did not have the physical body of a runner, nor did her heart rate indicate the rate of a person who just ran more than twenty-six miles. Initially, she was credited with the win. When it was determined that she had not run the entire course, she was stripped of her title. Witnesses testified that they saw her exiting the subway to join the race a few miles from the end of the course. So we see a person trying to claim glory in the victory, even though she did not have the right. She stole the glory from the rightful owner.

When we serve others through Christ, we are to remember who has supplied us with all our abilities and the opportunity to serve. We must avoid such "marathon runner" moments in any attempt to bring honor to ourselves. Serving others is meant to be an unselfish act of compassion and kindness, done in the name of our Lord. When we expect a "thank you" in return for our service, we have separated ourselves from God and robbed Him of His reward. Even if we try to allocate a portion of a "thank you" to ourselves, we move into a territory where we don't belong. Every "thank you" belongs to God. If a "thank you" comes our way, it is our responsibility to reflect 100 percent of that "thank you" to God, the rightful owner.

Paul's letter to the church at Colosse puts it quite simply: whatever we do, we *"do it all in the name of the Lord Jesus, giving thanks to God the Father through him"* (Colossians 3:17). We have a choice to make. How much do we expect a "thank you," and how much of the thanks do we wish to absorb?

Reflections:

- When you have served others, did you view it more as serving God or serving the recipients?
- Are you sharing God's message in your works of service?
- How well do you reflect a "thank you" for your service back to God – for His honor and glory?
- What is your spirit guiding you to pray for?

CONDEMNED VS. FORGIVEN

*"Therefore, **there is now no condemnation for those who are in Christ Jesus**, because through Christ Jesus the law of the Spirit of life set me free from the law of sin and death. For what the law was powerless to do in that it was weakened by the sinful nature, God did by sending his own Son in the likeness of sinful man to be a sin offering. And so he condemned sin in sinful man, in order that the righteous requirements of the law might be fully met in us, who do not live according to the sinful nature but according to the Spirit."*
(Romans 8:1-4)

Never allow past sins to control your future. Throughout the Scriptures, we are shown that *all* sins are forgivable. So to condemn oneself because of a sinful past is not of God. Jesus' sacrificial death was for all: the good, the bad, and everyone in between.

Paul's story is a great example of how a horrific past did not stop God from using him in the future. Remember, Paul persecuted Christians, yet after his conversion God still used Paul to deliver His message to the world. Paul did not allow his past sins to control his future. In this way, he could achieve much and be useful to God.

As demonstrated by Paul's life, God is always ready to offer new beginnings to those who truly repent. So never let the past stop the life that God wants you to live.

> *"Like water spilled on the ground, which cannot be recovered, so we must die. But God does not take away life; instead, he devises ways so that a banished person may not remain estranged from him."* (2 Samuel 14:14)

Always remember God loves everyone who comes to Him, and with that love there is forgiveness. It is our choice either to accept God's grace, which is offered to everyone, or to be blind to His Ways.

> *"The Lord is faithful to all his promises and loving toward all he has made. The Lord upholds all those who fall and lifts up all who are bowed down."* (Psalm 145:13-14)

Reflections:

- Are there any past events that have a hold on your life? If so, now is the time to accept God's grace by allowing Jesus' death to cover your sins. Allow God to shed light on a new way of living for Him.
- Is there anyone in your path who is allowing past sins to hold them back? Do you share the new beginnings that are offered by God to all?
- What is your spirit guiding you to pray for?

PANIC VS. CALM

"The Lord is my rock, my fortress and my deliverer; my God is my rock, in whom I take refuge, my shield and the horn of my salvation." (2 Samuel 22:2-3)

I was watching a television show in which a deck-hand on a crab boat described a terrible event that took place at sea. The boat suffered a mechanical failure during a storm. The captain and crew felt that the boat was going to sink, so all eleven jumped into the freezing Alaskan sea. Unfortunately, only two of the crew survived. The tragedy was that a couple of days later the Coast Guard found the ship still afloat. Had everyone stayed aboard, no one would have perished. That got me to thinking. During what times in my life did I choose to abandon God's way because I panicked versus waiting for His timing?

There is a difference between jumping ship when called upon by God to do so versus jumping ship in a faithless panic.

"When I am afraid, I will trust in you. In God, whose word I praise, in God I trust; I will not be afraid." (Psalm 56:3)

"I will take refuge in the shadow of your wings until the disaster has passed." (Psalm 57:1)

When times get tough, our best decision is to pray and listen to God to figure out if we are really sinking, needing to get out of a bad situation, or just going through a storm.

<u>Reflections:</u>

- Have you ever jumped ship before God had a chance to act in a certain situation?
- Has fear ever crept in and stopped you from pursuing an action that God put on your heart?
- When trials arise, do you tend to abandon ship before going to God for help?
- What is your spirit guiding you to pray for?

MINIMUM EFFORT VS. GOING BEYOND THE MINIMUM

"The servant hurried to meet her and said, 'Please give me a little water from your jar.' 'Drink, my lord,' she said, and quickly lowered the jar to her hands and gave him a drink. After she had given him a drink, she said, 'I'll draw water for your camels too, until they have finished drinking.' So she quickly emptied her jar into the trough, ran back to the well to draw more water, and drew enough for all his camels." (Genesis 24:17-20)

R ebekah is a great example of a motivated servant for God. Isaac's servant only asked for water for himself, not the camels. Rebekah fulfilled his request and went beyond the minimum by drawing enough water for the ten camels, until they had their fill. That was a lot of water and a whole lot of work. Also, notice her performance. She did not take her time. Rebekah *quickly* emptied her jar into the trough and *ran* back to the well to draw more water. Rebekah provides us with two great lessons: going beyond the minimum level of service, and going beyond the minimum level of effort.

To go beyond the minimum requires taking the focus from ourselves and putting that focus onto others. That is what serving is all about. As believers, taking our level of service up a few notches will allow others to witness our testimony in the Lord. Our effort must be unique. If we are the same as others, then our testimony is no different from everyone else's. With all that God has provided for us, serving Him halfheartedly is not a very genuine reflection of our appreciation.

A key "thank you" that we can offer to God is to bring glory to the kingdom by serving others in a way that goes beyond the minimum. It is our choice as to how we will represent the kingdom.

Reflections:

- Do you feel that you have been serving God at a minimum level or at a level beyond the minimum?
- Has God brought to light an area of your life that will require you to go beyond the minimum level of service and effort?
- What can you do beyond the minimum for someone this week? Consider doing it for someone you do not even know.

• What is your spirit guiding you to pray for?

> *"This is what Hezekiah did throughout Judah, doing what was good and right and faithful before the Lord his God. In everything that he undertook in the service of God's temple, and in obedience to the law and the commands, he sought his God, and worked wholeheartedly. And so he prospered."* (2 Chronicles 31:20-21)

TIGHTFISTED VS. OPENHANDED

"If there is a poor man among your brothers, in any of the towns of the land that the Lord your God is giving you, do not be hardhearted or tightfisted toward your poor brother. Rather be openhanded, and freely lend him whatever he needs. Be careful not to harbor this wicked thought..." (Deuteronomy 15:7-9)

The greatest commandant Jesus spoke of is love, and giving is a great expression of that love.

When we fall in love with our money and our possessions, they become difficult to relinquish. When there is a struggle for us to give up our posses- sions, we have developed a relationship with them. Regrettably, such a relationship leads many people into a false sense of security while in reality this relationship is unstable, and one that obstructs God's aspirations for us.

The Scriptures clearly point out that we cannot have both God and money as our masters.

"No one can serve two masters. Either he will hate the one, and love the other, or he will be devoted to the one, and despise the other. You cannot serve both God and Money." (Matthew 6:24)

God and money pull in opposite directions. To believe otherwise is to delude ourselves. If God lays a situation upon your heart to give, but your earthly response is "I need this money," you can easily see that these two masters work in opposite directions. To love money and to be a generous giver is like trying to mix oil and water. They just don't mix.

God will test us to see where our heart stands with Him. In Genesis 22, we see Abraham passing God's test. He was willing to sacrifice to God his greatest possession, his son Isaac. Then in Matthew 19:16-22 we read of the rich young man who failed God's test because he could only follow commandments five through ten. He could not follow the first and greatest commandment – having a personal relationship with God. We see this rich young man walking away sadly because he was so tied to his wealth that he could not relinquish it for a relationship with God.

The bottom line is that you can't love money and be in a blessed relationship with God. You must choose to whom you will be devoted. To be with God requires openhandedness. It is just impossible for a hand to be both tightfisted and openhanded at the same time.

Reflections:

- Does your checkbook reflect the heart of a giver or that of a hoarder?
- How do you handle situations when deciding to give or not to give?
- How well do you pay off your vows to give?
- Does your money and possessions give you a sense of security?
- What is your spirit guiding you to pray for?

AIMLESS VS. PURPOSEFUL

"I do not run like a man running aimlessly…"
(1 Corinthians 9:26)

We are not to live our lives like aimless tumbleweed, blown by the wind with no clue in the world as to where we are going. We are to live purposeful lives under God's guidance.

"The purposes of a man's heart are deep waters, but a man of understanding draws them out." (Proverbs 20:5)

This Scripture informs us that our purposes in life run deep in our soul. Finding our purposes is like being on a treasure hunt. Treasure hunts are not easy, and they require a lot of research, a lot of planning, and a strong determination to find the treasure in spite of all roadblocks and letdowns.

In order to find the purposes that God has in store for us, we need a spiritual plan. Such a plan incorporates things like daily reading of the Scriptures, prayer, fasting, serving others, offerings, worship, fellowship, etc. Additionally, as with any treasure hunt, we need to stay focused, be patient, and have an enduring determination to find our spiritual purposes. It could be years before God reveals them to us.

If your purposes have not been revealed, keep seeking. Those purposes will be revealed at some point. You may not be ready spiritually for the mission God has for you. A caterpillar cannot fly until it becomes a butterfly. Just remain faithful, because that day will come when your mission will be revealed. Remember the purposes are deep, and your effort to find them will prepare you to carry them out successfully. The bottom line is not to limp around aimlessly in order to find your purposes. Run in a meaningful way; it's your choice to make.

Reflections:

- Do you feel like you have spiritual direction in your life – a sense of God's guidance?
- Are you living life in a purposeful spiritual way?
- Do you need to improve your efforts in seeking God's direction?
- Has God laid a passion or purpose on your heart which you have yet to act on in a purposeful way?
- What is your spirit guiding you to pray for?

FEAR VS. COURAGE

"...the hand of the Lord my God was on me, I took courage..." (Ezra 7:28)

God has seen all – from the worst to the best – and has successfully handled it all, as witnessed throughout the Scriptures. So it makes no sense to allow fear (except for the respectful fear of God) to latch onto one's faith. Fear of earthly circumstances has a tremendous negative pull on one's faith. In Mark 4:40, we see Jesus making His disciples aware of their fear, and He linked that fear to their faith.

"He said to his disciples, 'Why are you so afraid? Do you still have no faith?'"

When fear begins to mix with our faith, our *actions* begin to override our belief in an almighty God. Not a good message to convey to nonbelievers. If I was a nonbeliever and witnessed a believer running fearfully, I would wonder "Just how big is this almighty God in whom they believe?"

My favorite movie scene is in the *Wizard of Oz*. The wizard spooks the lion, and due to the lion's lack of courage he freaks out, goes running down the hallway, and jumps out a window. Fortunately, by the end of the movie the lion demonstrates that he has triumphed over his fear and receives a necklace of courage from the wizard. God has a necklace of courage waiting for us as well. We just have to choose to accept His gift of courage, wear it, and trust with all our heart that He is always with us, and that His way will always prevail. With that said, what is there to fear?

> *"For God did not give us a spirit of timidity, but a spirit of power…"* (2 Timothy 1:7)

If you ever find yourself in the grasp of fear, admit it and seek God, because He will hear your prayers and guide you to the land of courage.

> *"I sought the Lord, and he answered me; he delivered me from all my fears."* (Psalm 34:4)

Reflections:

- Do your *actions* demonstrate that you are more fearful or responsive to the spirit of courage that empowers you to do God's will?

- Is there an area of your ministry or spiritual calling in which fear has created a roadblock and stopped you from moving forward?
- Is there someone in your path whose fear is overriding courage? Can you share some of God's wisdom?
- What is your spirit guiding you to pray for?

SITTING IN THE BLEACHERS VS. TAKING THE FIELD

"Each one should use whatever gift he has received to serve others, faithfully administering God's grace in its various forms."
(1 Peter 4:10)

God commands everyone to serve faithfully, while administering His grace. Unfortunately, too many people use numerous excuses not to serve God. They say they are too busy, or they feel inadequate, or they have other things to do, or they are too this or too that. They have become entangled in worldly things, causing them to become "excuse connoisseurs," which leads them to service immobility. When one becomes consumed with this world, it is difficult to overcome the excuses.

I wonder about those who confess their belief in Jesus but have no ongoing deeds to reflect such a confession. They claim that their lives have changed, but the way they continue to live their lives indicates that nothing has changed. They remain relatively inactive to answer the call *to serve others, faithfully administering God's grace in its various forms.*

> *"As the body without the spirit is dead, so faith without deeds is dead."* (James 2:26)

At sporting events, we see two types of people: those participating in the game and those watching from the bleachers. I wonder how many Christians are sitting in the bleachers just watching all the other Christians serving, as God intended. Being in the bleachers is unacceptable because we are designed *to serve others.* We are to deploy our confession of faith and knowledge of God into a ministry that glorifies Him. It is our choice either to act on our purpose for being created by playing on His field, or to remain sitting in the bleachers watching others doing God's work. Don't think about "I don't have this or that." Make the choice that states *I do have* an almighty God who created all and can deliver all. The bottom line is that all of us have some sort of ability to serve, so don't get caught sitting in the bleachers; answer the call to *play ball.*

> *"They claim to know God, but by their actions, they deny him."* (Titus 1:16)

Reflections:

- Is your walk with the Lord limited to Sunday services?
- Are you serving God in a meaningful way, or are you more of an observer in the bleachers?
- Since your confession of faith, has your "walk" changed, or are you still living life basically the same way?
- What is your spirit guiding you to pray for?

"You see that a person is justified by what he does, and not by faith alone." (James 2:24)

HIDDEN VS. SEEN

*"I will praise you, O Lord, with all my heart;
I will tell of all your wonders."* (Psalm 9:1)

Your faith is meant to be public, not private. We are to be a light to the world, not a light hidden under a bowl. However, when we speak of our faith, it must be done with sensitivity and in a non-confrontational manner. We are not to act like drill sergeants, getting into the faces of those who have not made a confession of faith.

*"Be wise in the way you act toward outsiders;
make the most of every opportunity. Let your
conversation be always full of grace, sea-
soned with salt, so that you may know how to
answer everyone."* (Colossians 4:5-6)

On the flipside, never be shy or embarrassed about sharing your faith. We have a great and mighty God who provides us with love and meets all our needs; so how can you not be motivated to share His ways?

*"I do not seal my lips, as you know, O Lord.
I do not hide your righteousness in my heart;
I speak of your faithfulness and salvation."*
(Psalm 40:9-10)

By sharing the joy, peace, faithfulness, and salvation that God has brought into your life, your testimony will allow others an opportunity to experience what you have received.

As you share your faith, just be yourself and speak from the heart. Each of us possesses different personalities, so each of us will have different ways of sharing our faith. There is no preset format to follow. Just be real, be sincere, and that will allow you to be a light to the world. I know it works, because that is how Pastor Rich Pennington Jr. led me back to Christ. Rich was real, sincere, and ready to speak the truth when I inquired. It is our choice to be a light that shines or a light that is hidden.

Reflections:

- How bright is your light to the world? Are you more hidden, or do you shine?
- Do you feel that you need to speak more about your faith?
- Do you feel timid in defending your faith?
- If you do defend your faith, are you confrontational or more sensitive in your responses?
- What is your spirit guiding you to pray for?

DISCOURAGEMENT VS. ENCOURAGEMENT

"Judas and Silas, who themselves were prophets, said much to encourage and strengthen the brothers." (Acts 15:32)

S erving God has its challenges. This can be very shocking to those who expect that ministry will be all peaches and cream. Those with such high hopes will be in for a rude awakening. Even though ministry is the most rewarding service we will ever perform, be prepared for challenging times.

The Scriptures tells us of the many individuals who suffered for their faith. The great prophets Elijah, Jeremiah, and Daniel were all persecuted for their beliefs. And of course Jesus, a man who led a perfect life, served the poor, served the downtrodden, and healed the sick only to end up being falsely persecuted and brutally killed.

Ministry will have its tough challenges, and all of us have a very important role to play. We should be in our watchtowers, scanning the fields for those fellow brothers and sisters of Christ who are caught up in the moment of the evil one's wrath. When we spot such a person in need, we must mobilize and swoop in to offer support.

One of the most important actions we can take is to use that most potent of instruments God gave us to help others—our tongue! On the tip of our tongue should be words of encouragement that have the power to lift another's spirit. To do anything less is to be a discouraging spirit.

> *"And let us consider how we may spur one another on toward love and good deeds."*
> (Hebrews 10:24)

If you are looking for a great role model of encouragement, you will find one in Joseph, also known as Barnabas. He so greatly encouraged the Christians in Jerusalem that they called him the "Son of Encouragement." His encouragement to Christians was so powerful it even moved non-Christians to become believers. Wow! It's difficult not to become excited and implement Joseph's exemplary ways into our own lives.

Never downplay the impact that your inspiring words of encouragement can have on another's life. Barnabas, who was a great encourager to both Paul and Mark, inspired them to keep persevering in their faith. The results of such encouragement can be read in their many contributions to the New Testament. And for those not of faith, your words of encouragement may just move them to become believers. It is your choice either to encourage others or not.

Reflections:

- Do you see yourself as a source of encourage-ment to others? Reflecting upon the last few weeks, how many times do you think you offered up words of encouragement?
- Is there someone in your path right now who needs encouragement?
- Do you use the Scriptures as a means to encourage others?
- Do you more often encourage or more often criticize?
- What is your spirit guiding you to pray for?

SEPARATED VS. TOGETHER

"Blessed is the man who listens to me, watching daily at my doors, waiting at my doorway. For whoever finds me finds life and receives favor from the Lord." (Proverbs 8:34-35)

I find it difficult to believe that any married person would say, "I have such a wonderful relationship with my spouse, because I give him/her every ounce of energy I have, and they give absolutely nothing back." A great marriage is one in which each spouse gives everything they have to the other. Marriage is a two-way street! Well, God wants the same: a personal, two-way relationship with each one of us. Obviously, there is no relationship when only one person is putting in all the effort.

David is a great example of a person wanting to connect with God in a personal way. We see God acknowledging this by saying that David was a man after His own heart. With David, we have a great example to follow:

> *"I have found David son of Jesse a man after my own heart; he will do everything I want him to do."* (Acts 13:22)

David had his faults, as we all do, but he also had this incredible passion to have a Father-and-son relationship with God. We read about this passion in David's confessions, through his repentance, through his pleas, through his rejoicing, through his worship, through his praise, though his questions, through his affirmations of trust, through his statements of confidence, through his thankfulness, and through his actions of loyalty. Place all of the above into one pot and you have a fabulous recipe for a relationship.

The bottom line is that God desires an amazing relationship with each of us. After all, we are to call Him Father, not Your Majesty, not King God, just Father. God will never be an absentee Father. He will never leave us or forsake us. However, for such a relationship to blossom and have meaning, we should not act like spoiled kids, *only* running to God when we are in trouble, or pouring forth a demanding tirade. Our relationship is meant to be an all encompassing relationship, as demonstrated by David, a relationship that is in touch *all* the time: during the worst of times, during the best of times, and during all the times in between. It is our choice as to which type of relationship we desire to have with God.

Reflections:

- Do you feel like you have a strong personal relationship with God – a personal bond?
- Do you feel that you can insert your name into this God-spoken sentence: *"I have found _____ a man [woman] after my own heart"*?
- How much time do you give to God each week reading the Scriptures and sitting in a quiet, uninterrupted place, nurturing the relationship through prayer?
- What is your spirit guiding you to pray for?

WORTHLESS VS. VALUABLE

"Stop trusting in man, who has but a breath in his nostrils. Of what account is he?" (Isaiah 2:22)

O ne thing I despised in high school was groups of social cliques. These people thought they were superior to everyone and felt empowered to assign a level of worth to each person. Unfortunately, such brazen egos continued beyond high school. We witness this in all kinds of global prejudices and from every level of society. However, we do have a fall-back whenever we are exposed to such judgments. God made us, and everything He made was wonderfully made.

"I praise you because I am fearfully and wonderfully made; your works are wonderful, I know that full well." (Psalm 139:14)

Never let the world determine your value. You can take pride in this. Stick out your chest a little, and when exposed to prejudicial situations say, "I beg to differ, for I am wonderfully made." God hand-formed you so you can feel humbly empowered by that truth. Never feel worthless as that is not of God.

God created you and He did so with a specific purpose in mind; you have value. So why would you ever allow the world to judge who you are? The bottom line is that everyone has value, no ifs, ands, and buts. Unfortunately, we will be exposed and subjected to those who have lost their way and need to bring value to themselves by demeaning others. We should pray for them so that they will see their own God-given value and have no need to demean another.

So never doubt your value or worth and what God can do through you for His kingdom. We see this with Matthew, who was a reviled tax collector in his society. However, Jesus saw value in him and said, "Follow Me." Matthew promptly followed and became one of the twelve disciples. Stay inspired as a creation of God's, and never speak the words "I have no value." You are wonderfully made, and thus you will forever have value. It is your choice either to allow this world to assign value to who you are or to accept the value of being God's creation.

Reflections:

- Have you ever allowed the world to determine your value?
- Do you feel valuable to God? If the answer is no, then seek some godly counsel. Work on your personal relationship with God, open your mind and heart to God, and allow Him the opportunity to reveal your value. Be patient, be diligent, and seek with all your being.
- Through God's eyes, are you living a life of value?
- What is your spirit guiding you to pray for?

CONSUMING VS. SAVINGS

"In the house of the wise are stores of choice food and oil, but the foolish man devours all he has." (Proverbs 21:20)

It cannot be said any clearer, a *"foolish man devours all he has."* When you are not saving, then you are consuming *way* too much; it is a choice you are making. This does not apply in all cases, such as a health crisis, a business crisis, or a crisis of similar magnitude. It does apply to most cases where no savings exist. However, if you are undergoing a crisis, the ability to save should have been present prior to the crisis. The bottom line is that God is not looking for excuses. He demands action and accountability.

"Jesus told his disciples: 'There was a rich man whose manager was accused of wasting his possessions. So he called him in and asked him, "What is this I hear about you? Give an

account of your management, because you cannot be manager any longer."'" (Luke 16:1-2)

To have savings you must have a plan, a plan that will yield results and may require you to go without some modern conveniences. A savings plan must come before you spend money on discretionary items. Before you decide to purchase a house, a car, a boat, or more clothing, you must have a game plan. You must first ask yourself, "Will such a purchase inhibit my ability to add to my savings and properly fund my retirement account?" It is your choice either to spend today or to set aside some dollars for the future.

"Now this is what the Lord Almighty says: 'Give careful thought to your ways. You have planted much, but have harvested little. You eat, but never have enough. You drink, but never have your fill. You put on clothes, but are not warm. You earn wages, only to put them in a purse with holes in it.'" (Haggai 1:5-6)

Reflections:

- Do you pay off your credit card balances when due, or do you carry a balance?
- Is your retirement account appropriately funded?

- Do you have at least six months, preferably more, of living expenses saved?
- Does your savings account increase *every* year?
- If you have determined that you are more of a consumer than a saver, what changes do you need to make today? What do you need to get rid of in order to downsize?
- What is your spirit guiding you to pray for?

> *"On the first day of every week, each one of you should set aside a sum of money keeping with his income...."*
> (1 Corinthians 16:2)

DISSATISFIED VS. CONTENT

"...I have learned to be content whatever the circumstances. I know what it is to be in need, and I know what it is to have plenty. I have learned the secret of being content in any, and every situation, whether well fed or hungry, whether living in plenty or in want. I can do everything through him who gives me strength." (Philippians 4:11-13)

I truly admire how Paul knew where his contentment originated, and it was not to be found on this earth. His faith and doing God's will was all Paul needed to be content. Nothing of this world had a hold on his heart. Paul learned the secret of detaching himself from any earthly desires in order to be content. Now, there is nothing wrong with possessing nice worldly things for our enjoyment, as long as earthly items are not *needed* in order to be content. After all, earthly cravings are temporary; a new car gets old, new clothes wear out, nice vacations pass by. The bottom line is that nothing of this world can ever provide everlasting peace in one's life. So why attach your ability to be content to such things?

We have a choice either to seek contentment within this fleeting world or to seek contentment in God and His ways, which lead to everlasting peace.

Reflections:

- Are there any earthly items, earthly desires, or even people controlling your level of contentment?
- Have you ever complained about your lack of earthly items?
- Do you find yourself to be more dissatisfied or more content?
- Do you feel you have *learned the secret of being content, whatever the circumstances?*
- What is your spirit guiding you to pray for?

> *"But godliness with contentment is great gain. For we brought nothing into the world, and we can take nothing out of it. But if we have food and clothing, we will be content with that."* (1 Timothy 6:6-8)

MISERY VS. MERCY

"Like water spilled on the ground, which cannot be recovered, so we must die. But God does not take away life; instead, he devises ways so that a banished person may not remain estranged from him." (2 Samuel 14:14)

No matter what wrong you have committed in the past, God offers forgiveness. This is clearly laid out in the Scriptures. With that said, you must also allow yourself to be forgiven through Christ's suffering and death, no matter what wrong you have done in the past. Christ's death was for all who believe in Him. You are saved by Him, and through His grace you are forgiven—not by your works. Not allowing oneself to be forgiven is rendering Christ's death as useless. That feeling of being unforgivable is the evil one with his foot on your throat, keeping you pinned to the ground.

Look at Paul, who sought and killed so many Christians. Paul saw his evil ways, repented, and became one of the most valuable servants ever to follow Christ.

The bottom line is not accepting Christ's death as a sacrifice for our sins. That is expressing that His death had no meaning – no use, a waste of time, a wasted sacrifice. God allows forgiveness for all who repent, so it is your choice to accept that gift. Make the choice that says Christ's death had a purpose.

"But because of his great love for us, God, who is rich in mercy, made us alive with Christ even when we were dead in transgressions—it is by grace you have been saved. And God raised us up with Christ and seated us with him in the heavenly realms in Christ Jesus, in order that in the coming ages he might show the incomparable riches of his grace, expressed in his kindness to us in Christ Jesus. For it is by grace you have been saved, through faith—and this not from yourselves, it is the gift of God—not by works, so that no one can boast." (Ephesians 2:4-9)

Reflections:

- Has something occurred in your life that makes you struggle to forgive yourself? If so, remember Christ died for *all* of us: the good, the bad, and everyone in between. Consider seeking some godly counsel to help you accept God's grace.

- Paul did not allow his past transgressions to affect his service to God. Are you holding onto any past transgressions that are limiting your ability to move forward in serving God?
- Is there someone in your path who is struggling with past transgressions? Do you need to share God's grace or help them seek godly counsel so they can be released from their bondage?
- What is your spirit guiding you to pray for?

"For the Son of Man came to seek and to save what was lost." (Luke 19:10)

EARTHLY PLANNING VS. ETERNAL PLANNING

> *"For our light and momentary troubles are achieving for us an eternal glory that far outweighs them all. So we fix our eyes not on what is seen, but on what is unseen. For what is seen is temporary, but what is unseen is eternal."* (2 Corinthians 4:17-18)

As a CPA, I have consulted with many clients regarding financial planning – earthly planning. For all the planning, there is no guarantee that it will work, because numerous assessments must to be made. For instance, the rate of return on your investments, the amount of money you will keep earning and the factor for inflation on your living expenses. Unforeseen circumstances can also mess up any financial plan. For instance, illnesses, a spouse's death, divorce, additions to the family, job losses, changes in the economy, global unrest, and weather disasters. Unfortunately, many people have focused only on their financial plan. Sufficient planning has not been given to what will be available to them for all eternity. It will be a regrettable day when the Lord calls and all you have done is lived a fleeting, earthly lifestyle. Fortunately, we have another option. We can choose to live a lifestyle with an eternal plan in place. If we live for what is seen, then that will be our sole reward. When we live for Jesus, we live beyond this finite existence knowing that *eternal glory* will be our reward as we cross over to the other side – a solid plan. So a decision needs to be made either to live like you have an eternal plan in place or to live for earthly means.

> *"For we must all appear before the judgment seat of Christ, that each one may receive what is due him for the things done while in the body ..."* (2 Corinthians 5:10)

Reflections:

- Is your lifestyle based more on what is seen or on what is unseen?
- Are there any earthly things your eyes are fixated upon that are hampering your focus on your eternal plan?
- How is your personal relationship with God?
- Do your actions and your lifestyle reflect living now for the earthly plane or for eternity?
- What is your spirit guiding you to pray for?

> *"We live by faith, not by sight."* (2 Corinthians 5:7)

WANTS VS. NEEDS

"The Lord is my shepherd, I shall not be in want." (Psalm 23:1)

I find it tough to listen to a child during the terrible twos, when they annoyingly demand "give me this" or "I want that." When they don't get what they want, watch out! The tears and the crying explode! Ugh! I wonder if God feels that way when we get into those types of "give me" fits.

For instance, how does God feel when He sees people buying homes above their means, becoming addicted to shopping, running up their credit card bills without being able to pay them off in full, buying a new car on credit even though the current one runs just fine, *needing* to have the latest and greatest of this or that, with no means to pay for it outside of credit?

The availability of credit has ruined many lives because too many people just do not know how to handle credit, and they have suffered the consequences. They have become immune to the ability to say "I can't buy that now because I just can't afford it."

Just a few decades ago, if someone bought something they paid cash. If you did not have the cash you did not buy it. Today, if you want something you just put it on your credit card. That is why during the past decade we saw the national savings rate become negative. Just think about that for a moment – a negative savings account!

So, as a Christian, what is the answer to this debt crisis? The answer lies in Psalm 23:1, *"... I shall not be in want."* It is just that simple. Stop allowing your eyes to control your pocketbook. Fall back to this blessing: that we have a God who *faithfully* meets all our *needs*, and for that alone we are richly blessed. Unfortunately, it is easy to get caught up in the things we wish we had—our desires. The danger begins when this festering of the things we *want* confuses us into thinking that such a *want* is now a *need*. This conversion of thoughts is dangerous. It can weigh us down spiritually, causing our thoughts, our actions, and our energy to shift our spiritual priorities.

Now there is nothing wrong with wanting the things of this world, as long as the *wants* never cross the line of turning into *needs*. The more we appreciate what we *have* versus what we *want*, the more we will realize how blessed we are by whatever provisions God lays before us. We just have to make the choice to allow our mind, body, and soul to come into alignment with God's ways and say, *"The Lord is my shepherd, I shall not be in want."*

Reflections:

- Are your prayers reflective of a God who meets all your needs?
- Do you ever feel that all your *needs* have not been met?
- Are you able to keep in check the difference between wants and needs?
- Have your *wants* ever interfered with your spiritual journey?
- What is your spirit guiding you to pray for?

FAIRNESS VS. UNFAIRNESS

"We must go through many hardships to enter the kingdom of God…" (Acts 14:22)

Many expect life on earth to be fair. The good receive their rewards and the bad receive their punishment. Throughout the Scriptures, it is quite clear that life on earth will not always be fair. Was it fair for Jesus, who led a perfect life, to be crucified for everyone's sin?

In times of tragedy, many ask, "Where is God in all of this? Why did God allow this to happen?" I cannot explain why certain painful events happen. All I know is that God feels the pain that everyone endures. After all, He had to witness the brutal death of His Son. Was that fair?

Paul learned the lesson that hardships are just part of life and ministry. Thus, he was able to block the unfairness in life from having any negative effect on his faith. In similar fashion, when we become exposed to such unfair situations, it is up to us to make the choice of viewing these situations as an opportunity to grow our faith or to disrupt our journey.

Reflections:

- Have any unfair life situations had a negative impact on your faith?
- When unfair life situations occur, do you use them as a means to grow your faith?
- Do you find ways to minister your spiritual gifts when others have had an unfair life situation occur?
- What is your spirit guiding you to pray for?

SILENT VS. CONFESSED

"When I kept silent, my bones wasted away through my groaning all day long or day, and night your hand was heavy upon me; my strength was sapped as in the heat of summer. Selah. Then I acknowledged my sin to you and did not cover up my iniquity. I said, 'I will confess my transgressions to the Lord'— and you forgave the guilt of my sin." (Psalm 32:3-5)

One of the greatest experiences I have ever had was to scuba dive at night. At first it was a little spooky, jumping off the boat into the ocean's darkness. If you have never dived at night, it is like sitting in a room without windows and then turning out the lights. You can't see anything, and this is what happened to me while underwater. Furthermore, I had no idea what was swimming around me. I had no sense of direction. I could not see my safety gauges. However, all this disappeared when I turned on my flashlight. The light gave me all kinds of clarity. I could see my surroundings. I could see the direction I was going. I could see dangerous situations and thus avoid them. And finally I could see my safety gauges, such as my air supply. You don't want to be 60 feet underwater and suddenly realize you just took your last breath of air.

Well, our sin is like the darkness of the ocean at night, and Jesus represents the light. When we neglect to repent of our sins, we are enveloped by darkness and we lose our sense of direction for a meaningful life. We become despondent and our senses dull. All this leads to a delusional lifestyle filled with excuses for misbehavior. As soon as we can get real with ourselves and repent, we will see the light of Jesus, who will disperse that ocean of darkness.

Our Lord's light overpowers all darkness, and through this light all is revealed. Darkness has nowhere to hide when light shines upon it. If we feel that we can hide or ignore our sinful secrets, we are extremely mistaken. We have an all-knowing God, and nothing escapes Him. Being quiet about one's sin does not make it go away. The sin must be confessed. Until the sin is confessed, it will assume power over you and become your master. God puts it this way: *"...if you do not do what is right, sin is crouching at your door; it desires to have you, but you must master it"* (Genesis 4:6-7). It is your choice either to be silent or to repent.

Reflections:

- Is there a dark area of your life that needs to be brought into the light, a sin that keeps repeating itself over and over?
- Does your history show that you learn from your mistakes, or do you tend to repeat them?
- When was the last time you repeated a previous sin?
- What is your spirit guiding you to pray for?

"God is light; in him there is no darkness at all. If we claim to have fellowship with him yet walk in the darkness, we lie and do not live by the truth. But if we walk in the light, as he is in the light, we have fellowship with one another, and the blood of Jesus, his Son, purifies us from all sin."
(1 John 1:5-7)

MOST OF THE MOST VS. LEAST OF THE LEAST

"Saul answered, 'But am I not a Benjamite, from the smallest tribe of Israel, and is not my clan the least of all the clans of the tribe of Benjamin? Why do you say such a thing to me?'" (1 Samuel 9:21)

When we view the world through our eyes, it is easy to put limits on what we can accomplish. We need to view the world in hindsight, by observing what God has done over the years. God started by taking nothing and creating the universe. God took useless dust and created man. God has continually shown us His acts throughout the Scriptures, by taking the least and making it useful for the kingdom. For instance, we see God leading Samuel to anoint Saul. Saul, a man from the smallest tribe of Israel and the least of all the clans of Benjamin, was to become the leader of Israel in order to deliver them from the hand of the Philistines. God did not direct Samuel to someone who had "the most of the most." He directed Samuel to someone who was the least of the least. Other examples: David conquering Goliath; Jesus picking ordinary men to be His extraordinary disciples in the eyes of the world. We see God directing Gideon to take only 300 men out of the 32,000 and with them defeating thousands of Midianites—and so on.

The common trait here is honoring God and making a commitment to see a task through. We are not to look at how much money we have, or how much education we have, or how much influence we have. We only have to look at our heart to see if it is willing to complete a God-given vision. God wants us to lean on Him and not upon our earthly capabilities. From there, God will provide all we will need. We just need to ask. Moses, who was slow to speak, asked God to provide someone to speak for him, and God answered, *"He is underline on his way to meet you...."* God knows what you need. Just ask!

The point is not to limit yourself nor allow others to determine what you can do for the kingdom. Currently, you may not have what is needed to complete a God-given vision, but don't let that stop you from moving forward. Go place an order of your needs, and allow God to deliver what you need. It is already on the way. In the end, the more you rely on God, the more you will be able to accomplish. The least of who you are may just end up being one of your greatest assets for the kingdom.

I never imagined that I would be a writer. I always struggled with writing while in school. To this day, I have difficulties expressing my thoughts. That being said, I experienced a situation at church one day that impacted my faith immensely. This experience was so powerful that I felt God telling me not to die with that experience in my head, but to put it on paper for others to read. So, not knowing the outcome, I started writing. It took three years of writing, rewriting, and many edits to end up with my first published book — in my eyes, a miracle. That experience led me to write weekly devotionals for a ministry I cofounded, and I am currently working on a few other book ideas. All of this would not have happened if I had allowed my weakness in expressing my thoughts to override what I knew God wanted me to complete. God took the least of me and made it useful for the kingdom. Making myself available to Him has forever changed me – and He will do the same for you.

The bottom line is, don't allow the lack of your earthly resources to override your God-given passions. Your passions will take you further than your resources. Just seek God, be faithful, be of pure heart, listen, follow His way, and He will provide all the resources you need. It is our choice either to make ourselves available to the Lord or not.

> *"So I say to you: Ask and it will be given to you; seek and you will find; knock and the door will be opened to you. For everyone who asks receives; he who seeks finds; and to him who knocks, the door will be opened."*
> (Luke 11:9-10)

Reflections:

- Do you believe that God can take the least of something and make it great? Your answer will determine how far you can go with God.
- Do you have a passion that you have not acted upon for fear that you don't have the resources needed to succeed?
- Have you completely closed off a section of your life that may need to be reopened?
- Is there a God-given vision that you need to put into action?
- What is your spirit guiding you to pray for?

"... I was not disobedient to the vision from heaven." (Acts 26:19)

SHOCKED VS. PREPARED

Our Spiritual Radar

"O God, whom I praise, do not remain silent, for wicked and deceitful men have opened their mouths against me; they have spoken against me with lying tongues. With words of hatred they surround me; they attack me without cause." (Psalm 109:1-3)

No matter where you live on this planet, at some point in time you are going to face stormy weather. A helpful device to spot distant storms is weather radar. This is especially useful in planning for hurricanes. Hurricanes don't just pop up overnight; they develop over a few days. Fortunately, weather radar forewarns us of these storms and allows communities the time to plan for them. If communities choose not to look at the weather radar to see what's coming, they will be left scrambling at the last minute to deal with the wrath of the storm. It will be too late!

Just as we will face some stormy weather at points in our lives, we are also going to face some emotional storms as well. As emotional storms approach, we should not be shocked; it's just part of life, and everyone will experience such seasons. We must be prepared in advance to handle such stormy situations. We must hunker down spiritually and gather our spiritual resources. If you are spiritually prepared ahead of time, then you will enter into the storm proactively instead of being in a state of shock and wondering what to do. Being prepared doesn't mean it will be easy to go through a stormy season of life; however, it will be a lot easier than walking around in a state of shock.

In Matthew 10:17 we read how Jesus prepared His disciples for persecution. He forewarned them and told them not to worry, He told them not to be afraid, and He told them that the Spirit of the Father would be there to guide them.

The Scriptures are like our weather radar. They forewarn us that forthcoming events in our lives will not always be happy ones. We are blessed to have these Scriptures as a resource to learn from and to lean upon. After all, they are the words of God. God shows us many ways by which others have successfully navigated through their stormy seasons.

The bottom line is that we can rest in knowing God will be with us. He will guide us, He will teach us what is to be learned, and He will bring us out of the storm in His timing. That is why it is so critical to make the choice to read the Word daily, to make the choice to pray for God's wisdom, and to make the choice to meditate on what God expects from us.

Reflections:

- Do you expect to go through some stormy seasons in the future?
- Do you feel spiritually prepared should a stormy season arrive tomorrow?
- When in a stormy season, do you look to the Scriptures to see how others navigated through their stormy seasons?
- What is your spirit guiding you to pray for?

I WILL TRY VS. I WILL

"I have taken an oath and confirmed it, that I will follow your righteous laws." (Psalm 119:106)

We should be very careful when using the word "try." When one uses the word "try," it immediately gives us an out for not succeeding. Our character and our testimony should not be tainted by the word "try." Our mindset should be "I will."

What sounds better?

- I will "try" to be a better follower of Christ, or "I will" be a better follower of Christ.
- I will "try" not to live by sight, or "I will" live by faith.
- I will "try" to be a better spouse, or "I will" be a better spouse.
- I will "try" to be better with my finances, or "I will" be better with my finances.

The bottom line, it is your choice to either say "I will try" or to say "I will."

Reflections:

- What do you need to stop "trying" and re-approach with the words "I will"?
- What is your spirit guiding you to pray for?

> *"I will hasten and not delay to obey your commands."* (Psalm 119:60)

WELL SAID VS.
WELL DONE

"You see that a person is justified by what he does and not by faith alone." (James 2:24)

"His master replied, 'Well done, good and faithful servant!'" (Matthew 25:21)

"Do not merely listen to the word, and so deceive yourselves. Do what it says." (James 1:22)

When you order a steak in a restaurant, the server asks, "How would you like your steak cooked?" What if someone were to ask God, "How do You like Your people?" By the looks of these Scripture passages, I would say that God likes His people "well done."

It is easy to say you are going to do this, or you are going to do that. Speaking requires no effort, and like the old adage says "talk is cheap." Speaking is a waste of words, and it is a waste of time for those listening to them when words are not followed by action. To hear the words "well done" requires works, not words.

When it comes to making pledges to God, you can say all the words you want; however, God will never be fooled. After all, He created your heart and He knows what you have in it. God wants our words converted into deeds. Like James said in the verse above, our faith is justified by *"what he does."* The bottom line is to put yourself in the position to hear the words, *"Well done, good, and faithful servant!"*

Reflections:

- Is there anything hindering your journey from being "well done"?
- Are there any changes you need to make to go from "well said" to "well done"?
- What is your spirit guiding you to pray for?

IT'S YOUR CHOICE
TO MAKE

"I love those who love me, and those who seek me find me. With me are riches and honor, enduring wealth and prosperity. My fruit is better than fine gold; what I yield surpasses choice silver." (Proverbs 8:17-19)

My prayer for you is that your choices will be in alignment with the Lord's choice.

CPSIA information can be obtained at www.ICGtesting.com
Printed in the USA
BVOW010932120911

270879BV00001B/5/P